Candy Hits

Candy Hits

by ZASU PITTS

Compiled by EDI HORTON

DUELL, SLOAN AND PEARCE　　　New York

Second Printing, March, 1964

Affiliate of
MEREDITH PRESS
Des Moines & New York

Library of Congress Catalogue Card Number: 63-16827

MANUFACTURED IN THE UNITED STATES OF AMERICA FOR MEREDITH PRESS

VAN REES PRESS   •   NEW YORK

To My Grandsons
RALPH and JOHN

Contents

A - ELI = ZA

N - SAN = SU

SU = ZA SU

Silent-Screen Days

Silent-Screen Days

Many people have asked me how I happened to choose candymaking for a hobby. It really began in my childhood, and if I close my eyes, I can still see the kitchen in our Santa Cruz home, smell the fragrant odor of spice cookies baking in our old iron stove and molasses candy bubbling in the iron frying pan that we called a spider. I can remember my mother's flushed face, her mouth puckered with concern, as she tested the syrup to see if it would "spin a thread," for she had no candy thermometer. How quietly I stood by, all eyes, waiting for that exciting moment when my mother would give me a piece of the taffy to pull into sticky strings, while she repeatedly flung her portion over a hook and drew it into a long, golden rope, feather-light, and easily cut by scissors. Oh, these were big moments in a little girl's life, until she grew old enough to make the candy herself.

Money was scarce at that time, and in order to hold on to our comfortable house which meant so much to my widowed mother and her brood of three, she was forced to rent some of the bedrooms during the summer when vacationers flocked to this northern California resort town. But as the winters brought extra hardships, it was necessary for me to go to work.

ZaSu with her sister and brother at her side

"You'll never make a seamstress," my mother said sadly, "you can't even sew a button on straight. But maybe you can become an actress."

I shuddered at the thought. Shy, self-conscious, my only interests were growing flowers, cooking, and finishing high school. However, Mother decided to send me to some friends in Hollywood who had written that young girls without any experience were being paid the enormous sum of three dollars a day by the moving picture studios. So off I went in Mother's best coat, dreading the ordeal that lay ahead of me.

On my first day at a studio something happened which

was destined to change the whole course of my life. I met
Frances Marion, who was writing almost all of Mary Pickford's screen stories. After we had talked for a little while
she took my hand and led me into the dressing room of
"America's sweetheart." I was so awe-struck that I stood
before this world-renowned star like a puppet on a slack
string.

"Mary, this is ZaSu Pitts," Frances was saying. "Don't
you think she would be a perfect casting for the role of
Becky opposite you?"

In the long silence that followed I was sure they would
hear my heart thumping. Finally Mary smiled and said,
"It's the part of a slavey—my best friend in an orphanage.
I think you'll be excellent. Now, what did you say your
name was?"

"ZaSu Pitts."

"Did you make up the ZaSu?"

"No, Miss Pickford, my mother did. She named me after
my two aunts, Eliza and Susan—ZaSu."

"A name people won't forget," Mary said, with a twin-
kle in her eyes. "Though I imagine many will mispro-
nounce it."

How right Mary was, for I have heard myself called
"Jazz-Su Pitts," "Shay-Zoo Pitts," and in France it even
stretches to "Sha-Sha Pootzie!" It is really pronounced
"Say Zoo."

The role of Becky in *The Little Princess* was the start of
my career. What actress doesn't thrill at seeing her name in
a newspaper for the first time? I did. Yet it wasn't exactly
a flattering review: "The girl who played the slavey opposite Mary Pickford, with the astounding name of ZaSu

Pitts, gave a remarkable and touching performance, though with her enormous eyes and thin, mobile, expressive hands she reminded me of a frightened little marmoset." I must admit that I cut out the latter part of the sentence before I mailed the review home, and underlined the "remarkable and touching performance."

Since that first meeting, there has always been a strong bond of friendship between Frances and me—not to overlook a large box of candy between us, from my own kitchen. Chocolate fudge was her favorite. "It's the best I've ever eaten," she said. "What's your secret, ZaSu?"

"I make it like ordinary fudge, but knead it like dough on a marble-topped table—when I can find one."

As time went on, my reputation as a candymaker spread, and I rarely went to the studio without my old string market bag bulging with boxes of caramels, panocha, peanut brittle, or chocolate creams. Friends brought me recipes, and I tried them all. Some were more successful than others —like my pictures, I might add. These recipes I tucked away, along with the ones I culled from magazines and newspapers.

Soon I discovered that whenever I felt blue or discouraged—for there is no clear sailing in any career—I found comfort and forgetfulness while I was in the kitchen candymaking. One day I whipped up enough candy to supply a whole studio while I tried to forget the greatest disappointment I had experienced since my arrival in Hollywood.

For weeks I had been working in *All Quiet on the Western Front,* and hoping with all my heart the serious role they had given me would further my acting career. While I had done a few comedy scenes in various pictures, Erich

In Greed

von Stroheim's *Greed* had established me as a potential dramatic actress. Then came the night of the preview of *All Quiet on the Western Front,* and I was shocked when a silly little comedy, in which I had played some amusing scenes, preceded this tragic war picture. The audience sat with rapt attention as the latter unfolded until I appeared on the screen. A gale of laughter greeted me. The following day the studio snipped off a piece of my heart when they snipped my entire role out of the picture.

Discouraged, I was packing to go home when Hal Roach sent for me. "ZaSu, you're a natural-born comedienne," he said. "The woods are full of actresses and actors who can emote, but there are few who can make an audience laugh.

Engstead, Beverly Hills, California

Now I'm planning to team you with Thelma Todd and hope to do a score of riotous two-reel comedies."

We completed sixty. And during that happy time when silence was golden, and on through that chaotic period when sound came roaring in, I kept on making candy for my old friends, and for the crop of newcomers at the studios. In fact, everybody began to call my morale-builder sessions in the kitchen "ZaSu's sweet moments."

However, I can recall many sweet moments that didn't take place in my kitchen; one incident in particular that made me the envy of all the girls. It was at a party where I blushingly admitted, when asked for a dance, that I didn't know the simplest step. As that young man turned away, a voice said, "I'll teach you, ZaSu." Wheeling around, I looked up into the handsome face of Rudolph Valentino! Ah me . . . so long ago.

But the sweetest moment was when the doctor said to me, "You have a beautiful little daughter," and laid her close to my heart. My Ann, who has enriched my life by giving me two precious grandchildren to love, to cherish —and to make candy for!

Four Basic Candies

When I arrived in Hollywood, I could make four different kinds of candy. They were basic candies. In that day every schoolgirl had her own special fudge which she used to whip up on a Sunday afternoon with friends. I could also make divinity, panocha, and I finally recalled my mother's taffy recipe.

Here they are—four basic recipes for beginners, but no matter how advanced you may become in candymaking these four will never lose their popularity.

Chocolate Fudge

2 cups sugar
¾ cup milk
2 one-ounce squares unsweetened chocolate
Dash of salt
1 teaspoon corn syrup
2 tablespoons butter or margarine
1 teaspoon vanilla
½ cup coarsely chopped nuts

I use a heavy two- or three-quart saucepan for this amount. It is ridiculous to use a kettle that is too small. An absent-minded candymaker can find her syrup boiling all over the range if the telephone rings or if she starts reciting the last act of *The Bat*.

Butter the sides of the saucepan. In it combine the sugar, milk, chocolate, salt, and corn syrup. Heat and stir over medium heat till sugar dissolves and mixture comes to a boil. Clip on candy thermometer if you have one. Cook till thermometer registers 238° F. Do not stir while mixture is cooking unless necessary to keep it from sticking.

If you do not have a thermometer, you must rely on the soft-ball test: Remove pan from heat; drop a few drops of fudge into a cup of cold water; you should be able to form the drops into a soft ball that flattens when removed from the water.

Add butter and let cool to lukewarm (110° F.) without stirring. The kettle should be cool to touch. Now add vanilla and start beating vigorously. Soon the mixture will become very thick and will start to lose its gloss. Toss in the nuts—I like toasted almonds, but walnuts are delicious, too.

You must gamble on that precise moment when your candy

Engstead, Beverly Hills, California

is about to "set up," and pour it out into a buttered shallow pan just before that critical split second arrives. You will then achieve a sheet of smooth fudge that can be cut in beautiful squares when cool.

My special variation on this method is that I pour the mixture out onto a marble slab or buttered board and knead it like dough, instead of pouring it into a pan. Then I roll it into logs, wrap it in waxed paper, and chill it. I slice it like ice-box cookies, and it is always fresh and creamy.

Divinity

Divinity takes a lot of beating, at least fifteen minutes of brisk whisking. If you have an electric mixer, you will profit by using it. Also your divinity will be smoother.

        2 cups sugar
       ½ cup light corn syrup
       ½ cup water
       ¼ teaspoon salt
        2 egg whites
        1 teaspoon vanilla
    ½ to 1 cup chopped nuts

In a heavy three-quart saucepan, blend sugar, corn syrup, water, and salt. Cook and stir over low heat till sugar is all dissolved. Then boil mixture to hard-ball stage. If you use a thermometer, it should read 250° F. Remove from heat, being careful not to disturb the syrup lest it crystallize.

Beat egg whites to stiff peaks. Slowly add the syrup, beating constantly at high speed. Add vanilla and continue beating till mixture forms soft peaks and begins to hold its shape. When it is the proper consistency, quickly add the chopped nuts.

I like walnuts, but pecans or toasted hazelnuts are good, too. Pour into buttered 8-by-8-inch pan, or drop by spoonfuls onto waxed paper. Let harden and then cut in squares.

If you have beaten the divinity an extra minute and it begins setting up too soon, quickly add a few drops of warm water; then pour it into a buttered pan.

Panocha

2⅓ cups (tightly packed) brown sugar
¾ cup evaporated milk or light cream
2 tablespoons butter
1 teaspoon vanilla
½ cup broken nuts

Panocha is not temperamental. If you happen to start daydreaming and let it cook a minute too long, or if you give it an extra few whips in beating and miss that split second of perfect timing to turn it out—just talk back to it firmly and add a few drops of cream. Your panocha will immediately cooperate; it will regain its soft creaminess and become perfect.

In a heavy three-quart saucepan, blend sugar and cream. Stir over medium heat till sugar dissolves and mixture comes to a boil. Continue to cook until a few drops make a soft ball when dropped into a cup of cold water. If you use a thermometer, it should read 238° F. Remove from heat immediately, and cool to lukewarm (110° F.). If you use the guess method, the bottom of the saucepan should feel comfortably warm. Add butter and vanilla and beat till mixture becomes thick and creamy and starts to lose its gloss. Just before it "sets up," add nuts. Pour into a buttered shallow pan. When cool, cut in squares.

Molasses Taffy

2 cups sugar
1 cup light molasses
⅓ cup water
2 teaspoons vinegar
2 tablespoons butter or margarine
½ teaspoon soda

Butter the sides of a heavy two-quart saucepan. Combine sugar, molasses, and water. Heat slowly and stir till all the sugar is dissolved. Bring to boiling and add the vinegar. Then cook to the light-crack stage (268° F.). (If you are using the cold-water test, the candy will be too hard to shape into a ball in cold water, but the firm ribbon it forms will bend when you lift it out of the water.)

Remove from heat; add butter and sift in the soda; stir to mix. Turn into large shallow buttered pan—don't scrape sides of cooling pan! Use a spatula to turn the edges of the candy to the center so candy cools evenly. As soon as it is cool enough to handle, pull the taffy—the hotter you can handle it, the better! Use only your fingertips; fingers should be ungreased; if the candy sticks, dip fingers in cornstarch. This should make enough for several pulls so that you can share the fun with your children. There's nothing like an old-fashioned taffy pull. When the taffy changes from brown to a light-golden color and gets hard to pull, cut in fourths; pull each piece into a long strand. Cut into bite-size pieces, using scissors dipped in butter. When cold, wrap each piece in waxed paper.

Talking-Picture Days

Talking-Picture Days

Here are the recipes that interested me during my busy talking-picture days. I think the more complicated directions in measurements and procedures are intriguing, and I pass on this information to the amateur candymaker who is still struggling with directions such as "Cook until syrup makes a soft ball."

Commercial candy, like professionally arranged flowers, has an easily recognized style. Often they both lack the charming individuality of a freshly picked bouquet from your own garden or some butter creams whipped up in your own kitchen. And candy tastes much better if you make it yourself.

Our house in southern California was as comfortable as my mother's old-fashioned one in the northern part of the state with its ample sunny kitchen. The heart of our Brentwood home was its kitchen, too. It wasn't square or oblong or L-shaped. It was round—completely round. It was my dream come true. Here in this unique kitchen our friends gathered. We were not gossips—instead those circular walls often echoed with a barrage of exchanged recipes. I collected rare molds to decorate the walls. Cookbooks filled special shelves and provided interesting reading. Imagine my astonishment when I read that even professional candy-making requires very little special equipment. Many famous candies were dreamed up in ordinary kitchens by dedicated women who turned hobbies into successful business ventures. All I wanted to do was to make the best candy I possibly could. The books said all I needed was a four-quart saucepan, a wooden spoon, a whisk, a dover egg beater, and a large platter for cooking candy. I glanced about me. Yes, I had countless saucepans of varying sizes. Certainly I had wooden spoons—some of them carved in Norway. Egg beaters? I had the latest electric one. I had cooky sheets and platters and Pyrex dishes.

I read on. "A candy thermometer is essential." The very thought of taking the guesswork out of "cook until the syrup spins a fine thread" sent me spinning out of that round kitchen like a top. I bought a candy thermometer immediately, and brought it back to turn my kitchen into a confectioner's paradise. I was in business.

From then on I learned to use a thermometer, and I learned to measure.

Candy Temperatures

Type of Candy	Temperature Fahrenheit	Cold-water test
Fudge, fondant, panocha	234°–238°	Soft ball
Caramels	244°–248°	Firm ball
Divinity	248°–254°	Hard ball
Taffy	265°–285°	Light crack
Butterscotch, toffee, brittles	290°–300°	Hard crack

With Thelma Todd in Let's Do Things

To use thermometer: Clip the candy thermometer to the pan after the syrup boils. Make sure the bulb is covered with boiling syrup, not just foam. Read thermometer with your eyes level with the markings, while syrup is boiling. (Before each candymaking session, check candy thermometer in boiling water. If it registers above or below 212° F. you'll need to add or subtract degrees to make the same allowance in the recipe.) Two or three degrees can make a big, bad difference in your candy.

To make cold-water test: Pour cold water (not ice cold) into a small bowl. Remove candy from heat while making test. Immediately spoon a few drops of syrup into water. Shape drops into a ball. The firmness of the ball indicates the temperature of the syrup.

Soft-ball Stage: In cold water, the hot syrup makes a soft ball which flattens when removed from the water.

Firm-ball Stage: In cold water, the hot syrup makes a firm ball which does not flatten when taken out of the water.

Hard-ball Stage: In cold water, the hot syrup makes a hard ball which holds its shape, but is plastic.

Light-crack Stage: In cold water, the syrup separates into threads which are hard but *not* brittle.

Hard-crack Stage: In cold water, the syrup separates into thread which are hard *and* brittle.

Equivalents

```
 3 teaspoons   = 1 tablespoon
 2 tablespoons = 1 fluid ounce
 4 tablespoons = ¼ cup
 8 tablespoons = ½ cup
16 tablespoons = 1 cup

 1 gill        = ½ cup
½ pint         = 1 cup
 2 pints       = 1 quart
 1 quart       = 4 cups
```

Table of Measures and Weights

1 pound granulated sugar	=	2 cups
1 pound confectioners' sugar	=	about 4½ cups (sifted)
1 pound brown sugar	=	2¼ cups (packed)
1 cup molasses	=	10 ounces
1 pound marshmallows	=	64 (regular size)
1 pound almond paste	=	2 cups (packed)
1 cup egg whites	=	8–10 whites
1 pint whole milk	=	1 cup evaporated milk plus 1 cup water
1 pound shelled almonds	=	3 cups
1 pound shelled walnuts	=	4 cups
1 pound shelled pecans	=	3–4 cups
1 pound shredded coconut	=	6 cups
1 pound butter	=	2 cups
1 pound vegetable shortening	=	2 cups
1 ounce unsweetened chocolate	=	1 square
1 pound unpitted dates	=	2½ cups
1 pound figs	=	2¾ cups
1 pound dried apricots	=	3½ cups
1 pound raisins	=	2½–3 cups
1 pound popcorn (unpopped)	=	2⅔ cups

৵ৡ

I was between pictures, and I was bored. I wandered around my gleaming-white, arena-like kitchen. A new French cookbook had just arrived. I flipped it open and discovered magnificent illustrations—boned chickens trussed up on elaborately garnished platters—soups steaming from colorful tureens—and the bonbons! They were irresistible.

As "Miss Polly"

An array of chocolate creams were presented like jewels. Here was my challenge.

There were drawings of hands in action—fingers so delicately sweeping pale fondants through luscious melted chocolate, the thumb and index finger so fastidiously holding a Brazil nut over a gleaming copper kettle. I glanced at my hands. Could they capture my dream?

I was off on a confectioner's cloud. An hour later my tears were washing away the chocolate smears on my face. My hands and arms were covered with a brown, sticky goo, my beautiful kitchen was a mess—my cloud had burst. I blamed it all on the fact that I couldn't read French. It was the only way I could save face; that and a hot shower.

Later in desperation I had the directions for *Bonbons au Grillage* translated into English. I then learned that *couvertures* cannot be made from just ordinary kitchen baking chocolate. This chocolate is very special. Professional candymakers can count on it behaving properly. Already I had learned that sugar is temperamental and I treated it with respect. But chocolate! Chocolate is the devil incarnate. It not only must be treated with respect—it must be catered to and cajoled into acceptable behavior. After that first exultant burst of enthusiasm the "bloom" was on my cheek—a dark, dismal chocolate "bloom." And beneath it, was my face red!

One beautiful, sunny day I wandered into the famous Farmer's Market in Los Angeles. I bought strawberries as big as hens' eggs and some fine cheese, and there, directly across from "Cheeses of Every Land" was a glass booth enclosing a sparkling candy kitchen. Two candy dippers, a man and a woman, were hard at work. I don't remember why this should have struck me as so excruciatingly funny, but it did. I think I had taken it for granted that all candy dippers were women. Then I recalled the French cookbook with its handsome illustrations of *Bonbons au Grillage*, which had been my undoing. It had insisted that a red-blooded Hercules was required to cope with the dragon, Chocolate. An anemic person might cast a shadow on the chocolate coating and the couverture would have a dull, gray bloom. I became fascinated wondering who had the most red corpuscles—the man or the woman?

The woman was intent on her task—her capable hands repeating the swirling motion through the glossy, thick, creamy chocolate—around, about, over—dab—a peak on top. The man's hands paused—around, about, over. He was looking at me with twinkling eyes. He finished the routine and the dab turned into a "Z." He was laughing now. He had recognized me. He pointed to the "Z" for ZaSu. I scribbled a note on my shopping list and passed it over the glass partition.

"Will you teach me?"

We both laughed hilariously. But that is how I learned to dip chocolates. I took lessons—professional lessons.

The capable woman turned out to be Mrs. Littlejohn, famous for her chocolate-covered English toffee. I became a frequent visitor to her shop, and she became my staunch friend over the years. Through her I met Susie Ribardier, who came to my own kitchen and helped me make holiday candies for my friends.

How to Master Chocolate Dipping in Ten Hard Lessons!

1. Pray.
2. Buy the very best dipping chocolate. I recommend professional coating chocolate, although it comes usually in not less than ten-pound blocks. Ordinary baking chocolate will not do. Use at least a pound of chocolate for a dipping session.
3. Don't attempt chocolate-dipping on a hot or a damp day. For best results, the room temperature should be between 60°–65° F. Take care to protect your chocolate from any temperature changes or drafts.
4. Buy a dipping fork if you can. Next best, make one from a coat hanger. Use the wire for a handle and twist the end into a loop to rescue and turn the candy.
5. Buy a candy thermometer if you don't have one already.
6. Place shaved chocolate in top part of a double boiler. In lower part, place enough warm water (100°–120° F.) to touch top pan. Keep water temperature constant. Melting the chocolate takes time—don't hurry it.
7. When chocolate is softened, remove from water and stir vigorously until the smallest lumps are all worked out. This creaming develops the texture of the chocolate, and you must repeat it often throughout the dipping.
8. Exchange warm water for cooler water (85° F.) in bottom of double boiler. Make sure chocolate doesn't come in contact with steam or water—even a trace can spoil it.

With Slim Summerville

9. Pour a cupful of chocolate into a small bowl or onto a marble slab. Work back and forth with fingers till chocolate feels cool—83° F. is perfect. Knowing when the chocolate is cool comes with practice. To test, let it string from the hand into the melted chocolate. If it holds a ruffly appearance on the surface for a few seconds, it is ready for dipping.

10. Dip away. Drop a center into the cooled chocolate, roll to coat, and lift out with a dipping fork. Scrape off excess chocolate. Drop onto waxed paper, right side up. As the candy drops from the dipper, twist the thread of chocolate to make a swirl across the top of the candy.

If the coating streaks, is spotted, turns gray, or "blooms," as the professionals say, a number of things could be wrong—chocolate too hot, too cool, too poor a grade, or maybe you yourself are feeling anemic.

The streaks or spots probably mean you didn't cream or mix the chocolate enough as it melted. Slow drying can cause streaks, too. Too much "base" indicates the chocolate was not cool enough for dipping, or the room is too warm for drying. If the coating is rough, the chocolate was too cool.

If the coating hardens immediately and stays dark, smooth, and glossy, you have followed directions perfectly. But for this first success, give all the credit to fate. You probably can't do it again right away. This is a delicate art, and can't be mastered in a flash. However, you'll continue to punish yourself until you are successful. Once your ambition has led you this far, there is no turning back.

Basic Fondant

Fondant is agreeable and co-operative in nature. It is as obliging as an old friend. It is a suitable candy contrast to the unpredictable chocolate that so often surrounds its gentle center.

I knew how to make fondant. It is as basic to a candymaker as the "little black dress" to a traveler. During my chocolate-dipping lessons my jolly professor laughed at me when I asked if he had a special recipe. "It's the same in any language," he said. I quote his recipe.

2 cups granulated sugar
¾ cup boiling water
⅛ teaspoon cream of tartar

"I can give you the same proportions in pounds or quarts or ounces," he countered. "It's always the same, but there are some secrets in the way you do it."

Tips for Fine Fondant

Combine ingredients in a two- or three-quart saucepan. Stir till every grain of sugar dissolves. Then place over heat and bring almost to boiling; cover tightly and remove from heat. Let stand for three minutes so that steam can wash down the sides. Uncover, return to heat, and boil briskly *without moving pan or stirring.* While syrup cooks you'll need to wash out the crystals that form around the sides of the pan. Wrap a damp cloth around the tines of a fork and wipe crystals out with an upward motion, so that no crystals fall back into the syrup.

Continue cooking till syrup reaches soft-ball stage—exactly 238° F. Remove from heat and let stand a very few minutes or just until the bubbles disappear. At once pour onto a large shallow platter, or better yet, a marble slab. *Do not scrape pan.* Let cool undisturbed till bottom of platter feels comfortably cool to palm of hand (about 105° F.). Now start turning edges of the candy in to the center, using a spatula or a wooden spoon. As the candy turns creamy and crumbly, gather mixture up in your hands and knead, using the same motions as for bread. You'll come out with a smooth, white ball of fondant. Wrap and store in a glass jar; cover with a tight lid. Let it mellow for at least twenty-four hours. I usually allow three days for fondant to "ripen."

Fondant Candies

Remove as much of the fondant as needed. Add your choice of coloring and flavoring; knead well to have uniform color and flavor throughout the candy. Shape in small balls; place on waxed paper to dry slightly. Now they are ready for dipping. Keep the fondant balls small, for the chocolate coating makes them seem much larger.

Nougat

It is necessary to make this in two parts; be sure to follow directions implicitly!

Operation I

1 cup sugar
¼ cup water
¾ cup light corn syrup
2 egg whites

Blend sugar, water, and corn syrup in heavy saucepan. Stir over low heat till sugar dissolves. Wipe down any sugar crystals on sides of pan. Bring to a boil; cook without stirring till mixture reaches 238° F. When the syrup gets to about 230° F. (thread stage), beat egg whites in large bowl till stiff peaks form. When syrup reaches 238° F., add slowly to the beaten whites, beating constantly. (Use your electric mixer for this step.) Beat mixture till very thick. Let stand while you do Operation II.

Operation II

2 cups sugar
2 cups light corn syrup
⅓ cup melted butter
1 tablespoon vanilla
¼ teaspoon salt
2 cups finely chopped blanched almonds, toasted
½ cup finely diced candied cherries, if you like

Combine sugar and syrup in heavy three-quart saucepan. Stir over low heat till sugar dissolves. Wipe down any sugar crystals. Clip on thermometer. Bring to boiling and cook to 275° F. (light- to medium-crack stage).

A portrait by Frances Marion

All at once, pour hot syrup over mixture from Operation I; mix well with wooden spoon. Add butter and vanilla gradually, mixing constantly. Now add salt, nuts, and cherries; mix again. Pat into two buttered nine-inch square pans. Let stand several hours. Turn out; cut in small slender bars. Wrap each piece individually, or dip pieces in dipping chocolate.

While this book was being written, I was asked, "ZaSu, where is your marshmallow recipe?"

"I don't have one," I replied. "I don't like marshmallows."

"Something will have to be done about that!" It sounded like a threat.

"Well, what do you want me to do about that?" I countered.

"Marshmallows are a basic form of candy. They belong in your talking career."

"They didn't then, and they don't now!"

"Oh, dear!" my accuser wailed. "Now I'm saying it. I'll be waving my hands next!"

I glanced at my daughter, Ann. She had been graduated from Stanford University as an English major, and I was relying on her to be able to cope with marshmallows.

"The boys like to toast them on Halloween, Mother."

"They can go to the neighbors, in that case."

"In that case you might ask Mrs. Littlejohn. She helped you out before."

Ann has always had a way of trapping me, of making me put my hands in my pockets. And so I did.

And this is what Mrs. Littlejohn, my loyal friend, adviser, and candy confidante, told me. She even wrote it out. When she handed me these golden rules, she commented,

Klein's Photo Lab, Culver City, California

In The Perfect Marriage

"Everyone likes marshmallows. They are even more delicious when coated with chocolate. Follow these directions
carefully, and I guarantee you'll have Candy Hits."

"But not by ZaSu Pitts." I thanked her, waved my hands,
and walked out.

Home-Made Marshmallows

2 envelopes (2 tablespoons) unflavored gelatin
½ cup cold water
2 cups sugar
¾ cup light corn syrup
½ cup hot water
2 teaspoons vanilla

This recipe takes an electric mixer. Soften gelatin in cold water in mixer bowl; let stand. In two-quart saucepan, mix sugar, corn syrup, and hot water. Heat slowly and stir till sugar dissolves; bring to boiling point but do not stir. Cook to 246° F.; remove from heat. Gradually pour syrup into gelatin in mixer bowl, beating constantly; this should take twelve to fifteen minutes. Add vanilla. Pour into 9-by-5-inch pan that has been lightly buttered and dusted with cornstarch. Chill till firm.

Turn out on marble slab or oiled board; cut in squares with buttered scissors or buttered sharp knife. Roll each marshmallow in powdered sugar or chopped nuts, or dip in chocolate. Store in tightly covered tin box to keep fresh.

Caramels

What is the secret of a good caramel? The best butter, the best cream. Both of these ingredients burn easily. Caramel syrup must be cooked slowly to avoid scorching, and the old-fashioned way sometimes takes several hours. Certainly all patience is gone by the time the liquid ingredients are evaporated, leaving the syrup at the caramel stage. A fine candy-maker confided to me her trick of producing a perfect caramel in minimum time. It's as magic as the old rope trick, but this one happens right before your very own eyes: *Do not add the butter and the cream until the syrup has reached 270° F. (light-crack stage)*.

Caramel Recipe

2 cups sugar
1 cup light corn syrup
2 cups heavy cream, heated to lukewarm
¼ teaspoon salt
¼ cup butter
1 tablespoon vanilla

In deep heavy saucepan, mix sugar and syrup. Stir till sugar dissolves and mixture boils. Cook to 270° F. without stirring. Now you need both hands and your undivided attention. Slowly add one cup of the warm cream—so slowly that the mixture never stops boiling. Cook to 250° F., stirring frequently. Carefully add remaining cup cream, about one tablespoon at a time, stirring constantly. Now add salt and butter. Cook to 250° F., stirring if necessary. Remove from heat. Add vanilla. Pour into buttered nine-inch square pan. Mark in squares, but do not cut through. When cool, turn out on a board and cut in squares with a very sharp knife or scissors. Wrap caramels individually in waxed paper or plastic wrap. These caramels should be eaten soon, for there is no added preservative. Their own deliciousness should more than make up for their lack of longevity.

Hard Candies

Mastering the basic rules of making hard candies is like having a skeleton key. With a few simple rules the inventive candymaker can produce lemon drops, jawbreakers, rum balls, lollipops, peppermint drops, or fill great glass jars with bright-colored old-fashioned hard candies loved by the very old and the very young.

By adding butter to the basic syrup in proper proportion you can have brickle or crunch. Add soda and peanuts and you will have peanut brittle. Change the final temperature and you will have toffee. Now for the rules.

There is a negative approach to the success of hard candy. Don't let crystallization occur! There are three rules to remember:

1. Do not stir after the syrup starts to boil.

2. When it boils, remove from heat, cover saucepan tightly, and let stand a few minutes so that any crystals that may have formed will wash down the sides of the pan.

3. Insert thermometer and return to heat. As the syrup cooks wash down the sides of pan with a fork covered with damp muslin. Crystals must not be allowed to form. Never scrape the sides of the candy kettle after pouring out the mixture.

Recipe for Hard Candies

2 cups granulated sugar
⅔ cup light corn syrup
1 cup water
  Few drops flavoring of your choice
  Few drops food coloring, if you wish

Mix sugar, corn syrup and water thoroughly in two-quart saucepan. Place on gentle heat. When syrup comes to a boil, remove from heat and cover tightly for about three minutes so that any crystals on the sides will wash down. Uncover, clip on thermometer, and bring to 280° F. without stirring. While mixture is cooking, wash down the sides of the pan with a fork covered with a damp cloth to remove any further crystals that may have formed.

Now reduce heat and cook syrup gently till thermometer reaches 300° F. (hard-crack stage); this gentle cooking prevents discoloration. Remove from heat and let stand until bubbles have simmered down. Carefully stir in flavoring and food coloring. For flavoring, I use oil of cinnamon, wintergreen, peppermint, or anise. Pour into buttered shallow pan. As soon as candy is touchable, snip into strips, then into tiny chunks. Drop candies on waxed paper. When cool and brittle, sprinkle with powdered sugar. Wrap, or store in air-tight containers.

Peanut Brittle

2 cups sugar
1 cup light corn syrup
1 cup water
2 cups unroasted (raw) Spanish peanuts
¼ teaspoon salt
1 teaspoon butter or margarine
¼ teaspoon soda

Combine sugar, corn syrup, and water in heavy skillet. Cook slowly, stirring till sugar is completely dissolved. Then continue cooking to soft-ball stage. Add the peanuts and salt. You can use Virginia peanuts if you wish, but you will need to blanch them first. Spanish peanuts don't need blanching.

Cook mixture to hard-crack stage, stirring constantly. (Remember to remove the skillet from heat while making the temperature test.) Stir in butter and soda—the mixture will bubble, but don't worry.

Pour onto buttered platters. Cool partially by lifting around edges with spatula. Keep the spatula moving under candy so it won't stick. When firm but still warm, turn candy over. Pull edges to make brittle thinner in center. Break in pieces when cold. Store in air-tight container.

Pralines

1½ cups medium-brown sugar
1½ cups granulated sugar
 1 cup water
 1 teaspoon vinegar
 1 tablespoon butter or margarine
 2 cups pecan halves

Combine the sugars, water, and vinegar in a heavy three-quart saucepan. Cook to soft-ball stage (236° F.). Add butter and pecans. For a deep color, I like to add a few drops of red food coloring. Remove from heat. Immediately beat till mixture starts to thicken and become cloudy. At that moment, quickly drop by heaping tablespoons onto buttered waxed paper or foil. Cool. Pralines are granular by nature, so don't cool syrup before beating. For uniform pralines use oiled or buttered praline molds.

Stage-Tour Collection

In Everybody Loves Opal *at the Pasadena Playhouse*

Stage-Tour Collection

My candy interests became conversational when my stage engagements introduced me to the straw-hat circuit. I went on tour on one-night stands and split-week billing. Sometimes we settled down for a month's run-of-the-play. I was always rehearsing a new play with an old cast due to the star system or an old play with a new cast due to a cautious producer.

On opening nights an appreciative audience flocked backstage to meet me. They invited me for lunch, for tea, for dinner. They were warm, generous people who wanted to share their homes and their hearts with me, a stranger in their town. Candy was a pleasant, easy, noncontroversial subject.

I read about candy in magazines and reveled in the beautiful illustrations showing new decorative ideas I had never even dreamed of in my own kitchen. I clipped recipes from the morning papers after scanning the reviews on the drama page. I felt that some day I'd put them to use, so they were tossed into my suitcase.

Here are some I enjoyed.

Chocolate Cherry Creams

1 cup semisweet chocolate pieces
½ cup evaporated milk
2½ cups confectioners' sugar
⅓ cup chopped nuts
⅓ cup diced maraschino cherries, well drained
1¼ cups coconut

Place chocolate morsels and evaporated milk in a heavy two-quart saucepan. Stir over very low heat until chocolate melts; remove from heat. Add the sugar, nuts, and cherries and mix thoroughly. Chill until mixture is firm enough to handle, about one hour. Roll in small balls. Coat with the coconut. Chill until firm (about four hours), and keep in cool place.

Coconut Kisses

4 egg whites
¼ teaspoon salt
1¼ cups sugar
2½ cups shredded coconut
Grated rind of ½ orange or 1 lemon

Beat the egg whites with salt until soft peaks form. Gradually add sugar, beating till very stiff. Fold in the coconut and grated orange or lemon rind. Drop from a spoon onto cooky sheets lined with heavy ungreased paper. Bake in slow oven, 325° F., twenty minutes or until delicately browned.·Slip the paper onto a damp towel, remove kisses with spatula to cooling rack. Store kisses in an airtight container.

Crispy Peanut-butter Bars

3 cups crisp rice cereal
1 cup salted peanuts
½ cup sugar
½ cup light corn syrup
½ cup peanut butter
½ teaspoon vanilla

Mix cereal and peanuts; set aside. Combine sugar and syrup. Cook, stirring constantly, till mixture comes to a full rolling boil. Remove from heat. Stir in peanut butter and vanilla. Immediately pour the syrup over cereal mixture, stirring gently to coat. Pat cereal evenly into buttered 8-inch square pan. Cool; cut in bars.

Creamy Opera Fudge

2 cups sugar
1 cup milk
½ teaspoon salt
1 tablespoon butter
1 teaspoon vanilla
½ cup marshmallow creme
½ cup chopped candied cherries

Butter sides of a heavy two-quart saucepan. Combine sugar, milk, and salt. Heat over medium heat, stirring constantly until all the sugar dissolves and mixture comes to a boil. Then cook to soft-ball stage (238° F.), stirring only if necessary. Immediately remove from heat. Add butter and cool to luke-warm (110° F.) without stirring.

Add vanilla. Beat vigorously until the mixture begins to hold its shape. Add marshmallow creme; beat till fudge becomes very thick and starts to lose its gloss. Quickly stir in cherries and spread in a buttered shallow pan. Score in squares while warm. Cut when firm.

Sour-cream Fudge

2 cups sugar
½ teaspoon salt
1 cup dairy sour cream
2 tablespoons butter
½ cup broken pecans

Combine sugar, salt, and sour cream. Cook, stirring occasionally, to soft-ball stage (236° F.). Add butter. Cool at room temperature, without stirring, till lukewarm (110° F.). Beat till mixture loses gloss; add nuts. Spread in buttered 8-by-8-by-2-inch pan. When firm, cut in squares. This will make about twenty-four pieces.

In the stage production of The Bat

Marshmallow Fudge

4 cups sugar
1 14½-ounce can evaporated milk
1 cup butter or margarine
1 12-ounce package semisweet chocolate pieces
1 pint marshmallow creme
1 teaspoon vanilla
1 cup broken walnuts

Butter sides of a heavy three-quart saucepan. Combine the sugar, evaporated milk, and butter. Cook over medium heat to soft-ball stage (236° F.), stirring often. Remove from heat; stir in remaining ingredients. Pour into buttered 13-by-9-inch pan. Score in squares while warm; if you want to be fancy, top each square with a walnut half. Cut when firm.

Fudge by another recipe

No schoolgirl ever made fudge like this—this is for the sophisticated!

¾ cup broken walnuts
2 cups sugar
1 cup evaporated milk
¼ teaspoon salt
1 12-ounce package (2 cups) semisweet chocolate pieces
1 teaspoon vanilla
2 cups tiny marshmallows

Sprinkle the nuts evenly over the bottom of a buttered nine-inch square pan. Butter the sides of a heavy two-quart saucepan. In it combine sugar, milk, and salt. Heat and stir till sugar is dissolved. Bring to rolling boil and boil two minutes, stirring often so mixture doesn't stick. If you use a thermometer, it should reach 222° F. Remove from heat. Right away stir in the chocolate pieces and the vanilla. Beat till chocolate is melted and blended. Cover nuts with half of this fudge mixture. Top with the tiny marshmallows, pressing them gently into the fudge. Now spread with the remaining fudge. Chill. Cut in squares. I place each candy in a fluted paper and pack in single-layer trays. It is even better if it is seasoned for two or three days—that is, if you can wait.

Television Days

Television Days

While I enjoyed my stage tours, I was grateful for television when it brought me back to my home in California. True, I worked in the studios all day when I was under contract, but I was able to be home every night. Sometimes I flew to New York for a special broadcast, but my life centered around my own fireside most of the year. There were always summer tours when a good play turned up. There were moving pictures when a good part turned up. I was emancipated—I was a free-lance actress.

Television also brought me the gift of new friends and of reclaiming old ones. We are a busy group here in Hollywood, and I find that the friends I enjoy most are the busiest—certainly the most interesting. We resort to time-savers and often get together for small dinner parties at one another's homes. I invented a new dessert which I often bring with me to present to a busy hostess and which is not only appreciated by her but also by her guests.

I candy dried fruits, stuff them with various combinations of nuts, fondants, marzipan, or even cream cheese, and roll them in powdered sugar, ground coconut, or ground chocolate. I arrange them individually in fluted paper candy cups and pack them in flat trays. If they are

ZaSu with her grandsons, John (left) and Ralph

stored in tight tin boxes they will keep quite a long time. On the other hand, prunes filled with cream cheese and nuts must be refrigerated or used at once.

They add tempting gayness to any coffee table, and there they are, awaiting the after-dinner coffee and allowing my hostess to bring her guests back to the living room after the main course of her dinner has been served. If it happens to be a servantless house this is a real boon to the cook who wishes to be in the parlor. If the party is composed of dieters—and most actresses watch those scales relentlessly—they are delighted to skip a heavy, fattening dessert. Men love these dessert substitutes, for I have yet

Klein's Photo Lab, Culver City, California

As part of the Day ménage in Life With Father

to meet a man who does not have a sweet tooth, and he resents being forced to go on his wife's diet.

I call my latest invention "Freeway Fly-Aways." I let my imagination go and make endless variations of these sweets that are so healthful. I've known enthusiasts to scoop up a few as they leave a party, rushing off to keep a late appointment for a television appearance or to see the late rushes from a day's shooting.

Dessert Date Snowballs

    2 18-ounce packages pitted dates
    ¾ cup water
    ½ cup flaked coconut
    ½ cup chopped walnuts
    ¼ cup sliced candied cherries

    Chop dates; add water; cover and cook over very low heat
about ten minutes or until the mixture becomes mushy. Stir
frequently. Remove from heat; blend in all other ingredients.
Chill thoroughly. Then shape in balls and roll in additional
coconut. Store in waxed-paper-lined tins.

Cleopatras

    ½ pound dried prunes
    1 pound dried figs
    1 pound dried seedless raisins
    1 pound pitted dates
    1 cup walnuts
      Confectioners' sugar

    Soak prunes overnight. Steam till tender, but not too soft.
Remove pits; drain prunes on paper towels. Wash figs and
steam gently for twenty minutes. Wash raisins. Put all fruits
and nuts through a food chopper. (I sometimes add a little
rum for flavoring.) Sprinkle confectioners' sugar on waxed
paper, or preferably a marble slab; knead confectioners' sugar
into the fruit mixture until well mixed and the fruit has taken

in as much of the sugar as it can. Roll mixture into logs; wrap in waxed paper. Refrigerate several hours or overnight. Slice as you would ice-box cookies; dust slices with confectioners' sugar. This candy keeps very well.

Candied Grapefruit Peel

1 large grapefruit
 Cold water
 Sugar

Wash grapefruit; peel and cut the rind in uniform strips, about one-quarter inch wide. Place rind in a saucepan and cover with cold water. Bring to boiling point and boil for five minutes; pour off water. Repeat boiling and draining four times, using fresh water each time. The fifth time boil the rind until tender, then drain, but reserve liquid. Measure peel and add one cup sugar for each cup of rind. Bring to boiling and boil till the liquid becomes a thick syrup (soft-ball stage). Lift out pieces one by one and roll in sugar. Let cool and dry.

Apricot Candy

¾ cup dried apricots
½ cup nuts
¾ cup shredded coconut
1 teaspoon grated orange rind
1 teaspoon grated lemon rind
1 tablespoon lemon juice

Combine apricots, nuts, and coconut; chop very fine. Mix with the orange and lemon rinds, and moisten with lemon juice. Shape into small balls and roll in confectioners' sugar. This will make approximately fifty small balls.

Glacé Nuts

    2 cups sugar
    ¼ teaspoon cream of tartar
    1 cup hot water
    ⅛ teaspoon salt
 1½ cups perfect nut meats

In a saucepan combine the sugar, water, cream of tartar, and salt. Heat and stir until the sugar is dissolved, then cook, without stirring, until mixture reaches 290° F. (hard-crack stage). Remove from heat immediately and place in a pan of hot water while dipping the nuts. Dip nuts separately with tweezers or with a wire dipping fork. Be sure to have nuts completely covered with syrup, then place on waxed paper or buttered slab to dry. Reheat the syrup carefully if it becomes too thick.

Note: To insure satisfactory results, the nuts must be perfectly dry. One drop of moisture can be fatal.

Jeri Toben

In the play The Solid Gold Cadillac

Glacé Fruits

Fruits may be glacéed as above; however, juicy fruits and berries should not be used, because of their moisture content. Use oranges, cherries, grapes, with part of the stem left on; dried fruits, such as prunes, figs, and dates are among the fruits most easily done.

Marzipan (Cooked)

3 cups sugar
5 cups almonds, ground
1 cup water
  Flavoring
  Food coloring

In a saucepan dissolve the sugar and water; add almonds. Cook, stirring constantly, until the mixture will not stick to the pan. Then remove from the fire and turn out onto a marble slab or baking sheet. While mixture is still warm, knead until smooth, and add flavoring and coloring.

Shape marzipan into flowers, fruits and vegetables of many varieties; color accordingly. This shaping may be done with the fingers or you may use special molds.

A MARZIPAN MASTERPIECE

An artistic friend taught me to make a beautiful tree
of lemon leaves bursting with bright yellow marzipan
fruits. It is decorative and can be used as a centerpiece for
a table setting either in- or out-of-doors.

The trunk of the tree can be made of an ivy log, with
twigs of lemon leaves inserted, and studded with toothpicks
to hold the molded marzipan lemons.

Marzipan (Uncooked)

    1 1-pound package of commercial almond paste
    ⅓ cup light corn syrup
    1¼ cups marshmallow creme
    ¼ cup fresh lemon juice
    2 teaspoons lemon extract
    ½ ounce yellow coloring (this should be added drop by
       drop, since coloring varies in strength)
       About 6 cups confectioners' sugar

Crumble the almond paste into a bowl quite finely. Mix in
corn syrup, marshmallow creme, lemon juice, and lemon ex-
tract; blend thoroughly. Add coloring a drop at a time. Then
knead in the confectioners' sugar, about a cup at a time,
enough to make the candy soft yet firm enough to handle.
Shape into small lemons—suit the proportion to the size of

the tree. Insert toothpick in end to give a growing-stem-like appearance. It is best to let marzipan fruits stand an hour or so before inserting the toothpicks in the tree, as it gives the candy time to set.

This recipe makes about twelve dozen fruits, more than enough for one tree. You may wish to box the remainder, or to divide the recipe; several different colors and flavors can be molded into various fruits, such as oranges and strawberries, or even into vegetables. Marzipans are delicious!

Texas Tycoons

1 pound (2 cups) butter
1 pound (2 cups) sugar
1 pound (3 to 4 cups) Texas pecan halves (I have tried other types of pecans and they are almost as good.)

This is a tricky recipe, so pursue it carefully and with patience. It can burn easily.

In heavy skillet, melt butter. Stir in sugar. Add nuts. Cook until mixture is a golden brown, stirring constantly but gently —do not beat. Remove from heat. Spread out very thin in a shallow pan which has been lightly buttered. This is a very unusual candy—brittle, crispy. When it is hard, I like to lightly salt it before breaking it into pieces.

Pirate's Treasure

This coconut candy is rightly named—the recipe is my greatest treasure. The candy is so delicious it should be kept under lock and key. It also improves with age when kept in a tightly covered tin. I pack it in pretty metal-hinged boxes I found in a ten-cent store, and they simulate a pirate's chest.

    3 large fresh coconuts
    6 cups granulated sugar
1½ cups coconut milk
    2 teaspoons vanilla

Grate coconut meat; in heavy saucepan mix with sugar and coconut milk. Blend thoroughly. Place on a very low heat. Cook gently until mixture becomes thick and heavy. Stir gently from time to time. You can test it by dropping a spoonful on waxed paper—if it holds its shape, it is done. If it is cooked too fast it may scorch and change color. Allow for *time* and *patience*. When it is done, add the vanilla. Drop by teaspoonfuls on waxed paper. Let stand till hardened. Pack your treasure in suitable airtight tins and await the battles for your loot!

Demitasse Sweets (or *Coffee Fudge*)

    3 cups sugar
    1 cup milk
½ cup light cream
    2 tablespoons instant coffee
    1 tablespoon light corn syrup
      Dash of salt
    3 tablespoons butter
    1 teaspoon vanilla
½ cup (½ of a 6-ounce package) semisweet chocolate pieces
½ cup broken pecans

Butter sides of heavy three-quart saucepan. In it combine sugar, milk, light cream, instant coffee, corn syrup, and salt. Heat over medium heat, stirring constantly, till sugar is all dissolved and mixture comes to boiling. Then cook to soft-ball stage (234° F.), stirring only if necessary. Immediately remove from heat; add butter and cool to lukewarm (110° F), without stirring. Add vanilla. Beat vigorously till fudge becomes very thick and starts to lose its gloss. At that moment stir in the chocolate pieces and pecans. Quickly spread in a buttered shallow pan or small platter. Score in squares while warm, and, if desired, top each with a pecan half. Cut when firm. Store in airtight container. This is delightful with after-dinner coffee.

Candies for Holidays

Candies for Holidays

Holidays are for celebrations, and all actors are adept at improvisation. I love to use candy to point up an occasion. I fall back on old and tried recipes and put new dresses and decorations on them.

During the Christmas season I wrap lollipops in bright-red cellophane, twist their pipe-stem handles into a holly wreath, tie it with a big red satin ribbon and hang it on our front door to delight my grandsons Ralph and John. They help themselves to a lick of cheer as they rush in to say, "Merry Christmas, Granny!"

Lollipops

  3 cups sugar
 ¾ cup light corn syrup
  3 tablespoons vinegar
 ⅓ cup boiling water
 ¼ cup butter or margarine
      Dash of salt
      Wooden skewers

Pete Klein, Hal Roach Studios, Culver City, California

Mix sugar, corn syrup, vinegar, and water; stir to dissolve all sugar. Bring to boiling and cook without stirring to hard-crack stage (300° F.). Toward last, cook slowly so mixture does not discolor. Remove from heat; add butter and salt. Let stand till mixture thickens slightly.

Place skewers on greased cooky sheets, five inches apart. Drop candy from tablespoon over skewers to make three-inch lollipops. To prevent cracking, loosen when firm but still warm.

On Valentine's Day you can make hearts—red, pink, yellow, green, and white, and the flavors can be just as suitably varied—peppermint, wintergreen, strawberry. They can be decorated with sugar ribbons and candied flowers—flowers from your garden. If you can become expert with a pastry tube, you can make birds and even inscribe little messages with a paintbrush dipped in vegetable coloring.

For Easter I make candy eggs of fondant dipped in bitter chocolate. These can be appreciated by both young and old. The decorations are as limitless as space and as fanciful as any mood.

Fondant Easter Eggs

1 egg white
1 tablespoon cold water
2 tablespoons light cream
1 teaspoon vanilla
5 cups sifted confectioners' sugar

Mix egg white, water, cream, and vanilla; blend. Add sugar slowly, beating, then kneading till smooth. Cover with a damp cloth and let stand at room temperature about 1 hour. Divide in thirds; tint each third with food coloring. (Nuts or candied fruit may be added to this mixture if you like.) Shape into Easter eggs. Now coat eggs if you like—use tinted flaked coconut, finely chopped nuts, or chocolate shot.

To tint coconut: Place 1 can flaked coconut (1⅓ cups) in jar. Add a few drops of food coloring. Screw on lid; shake till coconut is colored.

The Fourth of July is a perfect excuse to wrap popcorn balls in bright red, white, and blue wax paper.

Popcorn Balls

5 quarts popped corn
2 cups sugar
1½ cups water
½ teaspoon salt
½ cup light corn syrup
1 teaspoon vinegar
1 teaspoon vanilla

While you cook syrup, keep popcorn hot in slow oven (300° F.). Butter sides of heavy saucepan. Combine in it the sugar, water, salt, corn syrup, and vinegar. Cook and stir over low heat till sugar dissolves. Then cook withou stirring, to hard-ball stage (250° F.). Immediately add vanilla. Pour in thin stream over hot popcorn; stir just till corn is well coated. Rub butter on your hands; shape popcorn into balls. When cool, wrap in waxed paper or clear plastic wrap. This makes fifteen to twenty balls.

Treats for Halloween when made of candy may save tricks being played on you. When tamed with homemade candy witches will take to their broomsticks and fly away, leaving the good children on your doorstep to lick your candy apples.

Candy Apples

1 pound (56) vanilla caramels
2 tablespoons water
  Dash of salt
6 wooden skewers
6 crisp, medium apples
  Chopped nuts

Melt caramels with water in double boiler, stirring often till smooth. Add salt. Stick a skewer into blossom end of each apple. Dip apple in the caramel syrup and turn till completely coated. If syrup is too stiff, add a few drops of water. Quickly roll the bottom half of coated apple in chopped nuts. Set on cooky sheet covered with waxed paper. Chill until firm.

Then there are birthdays. One can give a history lesson by making honor candies to Washington, Lincoln, Franklin—molded heads made of marzipan mounted on chocolate plaques are a challenge. And don't forget the birthdays of your family and your friends. I keep a calendar listing them all, and can refer to the birth flower, the sign on the zodiac, and the special color for the month, and on short notice I can surprise a friend with "Happy Birthday."

Try initialing opera creams with the monograms of your friends, and tint the fondants the appropriate color, or top each bonbon with the flower for the month. Be sentimental.

And then there are all sorts of attractive ways to decorate the birthday box of candies. I have some favorites—all tasty, too—and here are the recipes.

Candied Flowers

2 tablespoons gum arabic
¼ cup water
½ cup sugar
6 tablespoons water
1 tablespoon corn syrup
  Flower petals of your choice—rose or violet, but don't try daisies. A famous and witty author warned against eating them, and she was right.

  Wash, dry, and drain flower petals carefully, snipping off the ends, which will taste bitter. Mix the gum arabic and ¼ cup water. Heat over hot water till dissolved. Now arrange the flower petals in rows on paper towels. Paint them very carefully with the melted gum arabic. This will stiffen them. I advise using a small camel-hair brush for this process.

  If you choose to do a lot of petals, try making strands of them—use a needle and thread and string them into necklaces. Be sure they are dry before dipping them.

  Combine sugar, corn syrup, and six tablespoons water. Cook to 240° F. (medium-ball stage). Let the syrup cool, then dip each petal strand gently in the syrup; set aside to dry. If you use great care the color of the flowers should be retained. They make delightful decorations.

Chocolate Leaves

Fresh leaves from your garden
Dipping chocolate or semisweet chocolate pieces

Select leaves from your garden. Gardenia leaves are excellent, because they are stiff and their undersides show the vein markings plainly. Rose or lemon leaves will do, too. Leave a little of each stem for a handle. Wash and dry leaves. Arrange on waxed paper.

Melt chocolate over hot, but not boiling, water. (If you use dipping chocolate, don't let it get above dipping temperature —about 83° F.) With a new watercolor brush, paint undersides of leaves with a smooth, thick coat of chocolate, spreading just to edge. Chill in refrigerator till set.

To remove leaf from chocolate, insert point of paring knife at tip of leaf, then peel it off. Now place chocolate leaves on waxed paper. Chill till ready to use. These are wonderful to decorate ice-cream or frosted cakes, or as a decorator's note for a box of candy.

A caterer told me that this is the method he uses for crystallizing grapes—great, luscious bunches of purple, red, or white grapes, which he hangs over the edge of a punch bowl resting on a bed of shining grape leaves. "Frosted Grapes," he calls them. They make lovely decorations.

And I found it equally good for candying mint leaves.

Candied Mint Leaves

1 cupful freshly picked mint leaves
½ cup coarse granulated sugar
　Oil of mint
1 egg white

Select young, delicate mint leaves; wash and dry. Mix sugar with a drop or so of oil of mint, and spread out in saucer. Now beat egg white till foamy. Dip each mint leaf in egg white, then roll carefully in the sugar, taking pains to coat both sides and not bruise the tender leaf. Place each leaf on a wire rack to dry slowly. This can be done in the sun, or they can be dried in a very slow oven. These are savory tidbits to nibble during a bridge game. They also make pretty decorations for topping off a crème de menthe sauce over ice cream.

Index of Recipes